The Groove Goblin

Written by: Saffire Bouchelion
Illustrations By: Christopher Creath

The Groove Goblin wakes
With a groove in his heart
Each day he is so excited
That he can't wait to start

He says there's grooves to be made
And every day is a song
And if He grooves deep enough
Others might come along!

Groove Goblin has everything
For the making of sound
Things you strike, shake and wiggle
Things you rattle and pound

But his favorite groove tools
No second of choice
Groove Goblin's best magic
Is his body and voice~

He grooves while he Gobbles
And he Gobbles as he grooves
Raises his voice to the heavens
Shakes his body as he moves

He next saw Sunbathing Sam
Already enjoyng the heat
Barely a pulse in his heart
Groove Goblin helped him find his feet

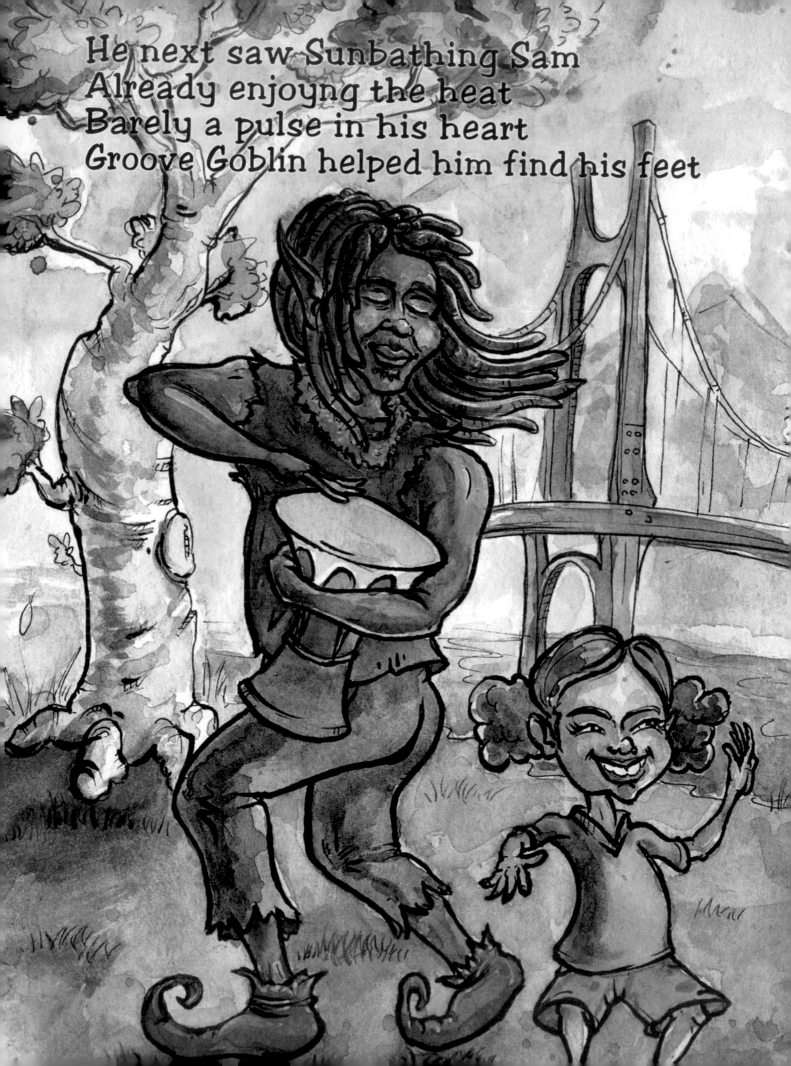

But Headphones Harry
Was oblivious to all
He walked right on by
And missed the Groove Goblin's call!

The Goblin of Groove Slumped
And thumped right on the floor
The Groove didn't reach the boy
Could he have done more?

When GG couldn't groove
In fact could no longer hum
He would sit and get recharged
With his lovely magical drum

And with the Earth's Heartbeat
Found within him again
He soon was quite ready
To go back out and make friends!!

Then he STOPPED
As he heard a most familiar sound
His groove friends had returned
From all around town!

Each was brightly and happy
Filled with their own Song
Joining in with their neighbors
Everyone did come along!!!

So

Always seek your own groove
Find it if you don't know it
And once your Heart is full
Do Remember to show it!

Because...

To chaos and mayhem
There truly is a solution
Let's all pulse together
And have a

The End

This story was written in 2 parts. The first part was written while riding a bus home from a children's camp I was teaching at in Singapore. The rest came into being while riding a bus to where I teach my dance classes here in Portland, Oregon. So the entire concept and text for the Groove Goblin happened on public transportation in 2 very different countries and cultures on opposite sides of the world. This is a fun fact but also very relevant to the story, as his whole mission is to bring all of the peoples of the world into rhythm with themselves first, and then with each other. It is my intention that his presence and his message make this world a better place for all.

Deepen your Groove!!

SB

Saffire Bouchelion is a 1st Degree Black Belt Nia instructor who has been passionately practicing Nia for 18 years. He is also a professional performer and musician. His embodiment and transmission of music and rhythm stir profound transformation in his students. He has taught Drumming, Embodying Rhythm and Dance into Being workshops throughout the US, Europe, Mexico and Bali for the past 11 years.

His greatest joy is helping to Embody the world, one Community at a time!

Saffireb@me.com
www.saffirebouchelion.com

Christopher Michael Creath finds passion & joy in a multitude of mediums, is heavily influenced by surrealism, and has an affinity for texture. With a passion for storytelling, he has worn the hat of painter, animator, teacher, and author of the children's book "The Boy Who Chased The Sun." Christopher creates fantastical surrealist landscapes and narratives with the intention of evoking thought, emotion, and creating a dialogue.

creath@brownbagstudios.com
www.brownbagstudios.com

40790679R00017

Made in the USA
San Bernardino, CA
28 October 2016